THE PRAYING ATHLETE™

PHOTOGRAPHY

QUOTE BOOK - VOL 4

Robert B. Walker

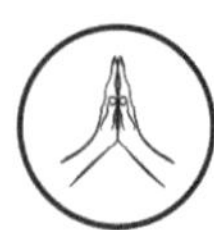

The Praying Athlete Photography Quote Book Volume 4

Published by The Core Media Group, Inc., P.O. Box 2037, Indian Trail, NC 28079.

Quotes written by Robert B. Walker. Photography by Robert B. Walker & Ashlyn Helms.
Cover and Interior design by Ashlyn Helms.

Printed in the United States of America.

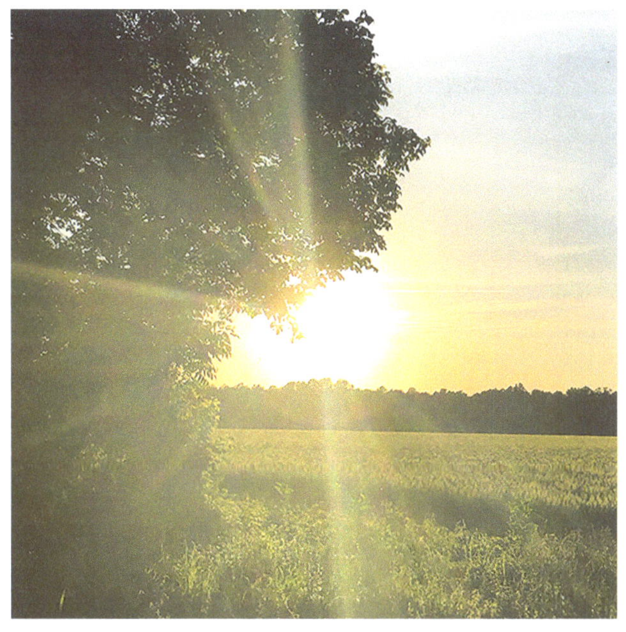

"What MORE can we accomplish before the next sunset? Give more, share more, pray more, trust more, honor more, serve more, lead more, hug more, talk more, empower more, read more, walk more, reflect more, love more."

"Without God's assistance and your persistence, there cannot be any pursuit to the dreams you have within."

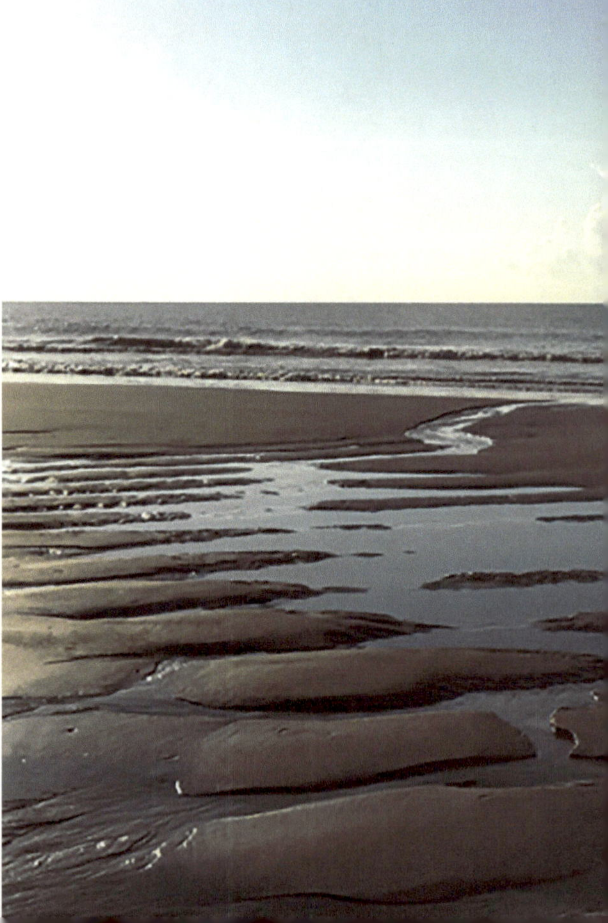

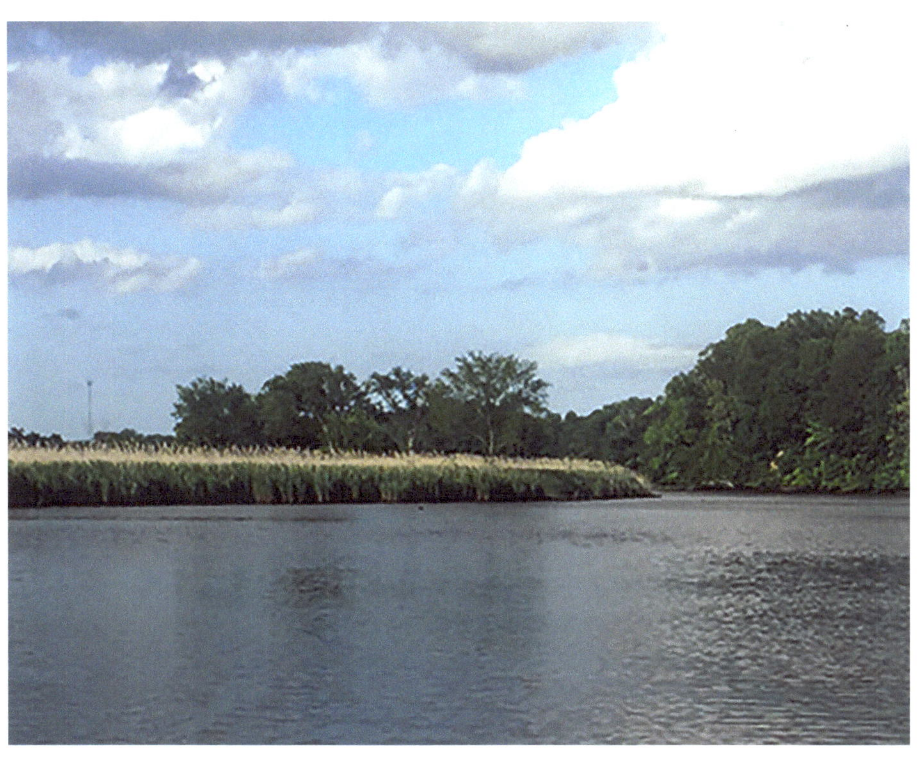

"Paddle, Paddle, Paddle. The engine of life you need is ahead. Never give up. The next island of success is around the bend—I promise. See you there."

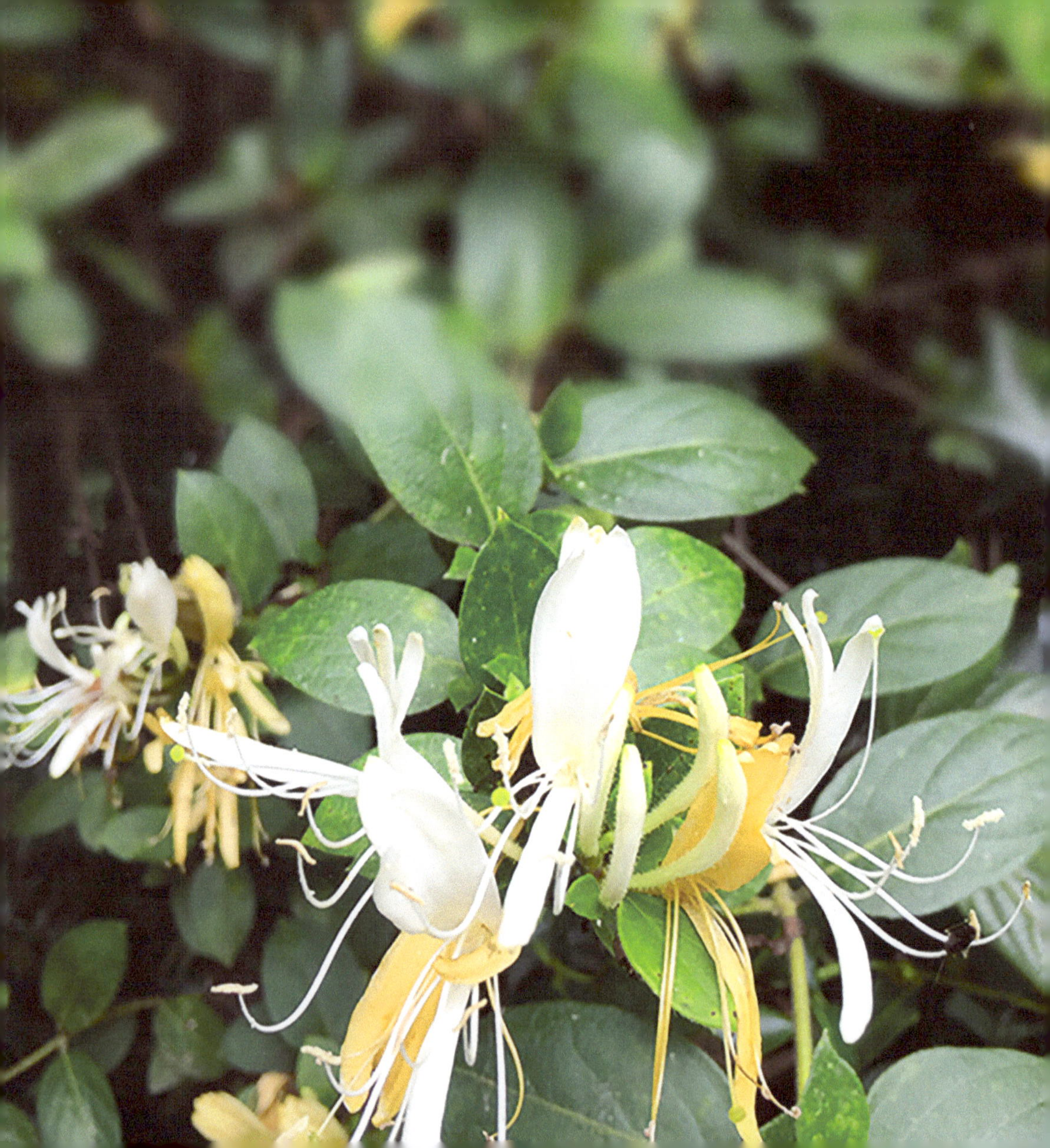

"Time well spent with Jesus will help us spread a beautiful fragrance of love, joy, and peace."

We are to God the pleasing aroma of Christ.
2 Corinthians 2:15

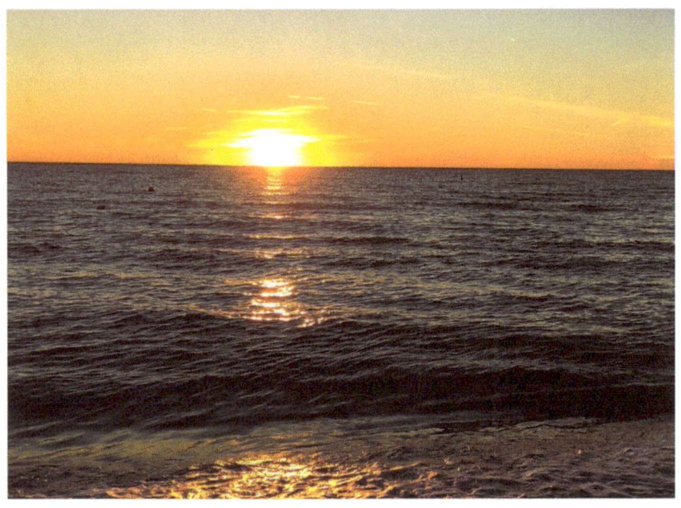

"Seeing God do this day in and day out gives tremendous confidence to know He has designed a very distinct plan. What we ask for seems so minor compared to the complications of the sun setting and rising everyday. Challenge God to bless you and ask Him to give you the desires of your heart. Aggressively attack and chase after His love for you and those you love. Never give up on the chase. Take a moment and look at the picture closely and follow the sun ray. It is coming right at your heart. The Son of God is shining on you and chasing after your heart daily!"

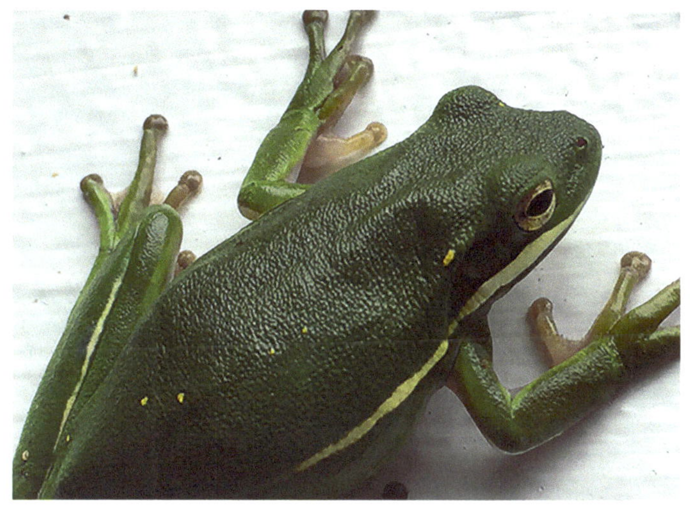

"Hang in there! Stick to it!"

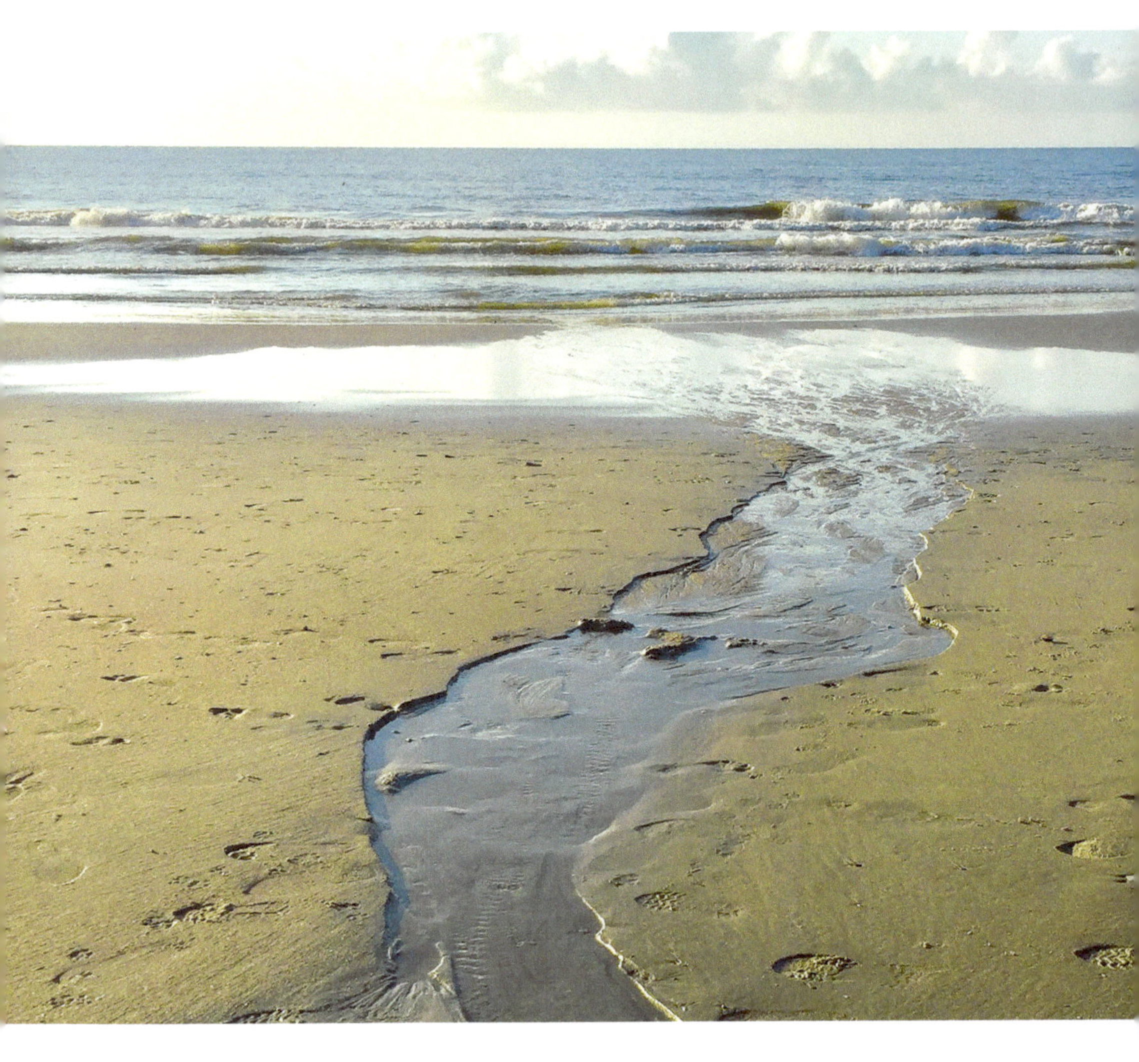

"Reaching your goals happens one way. Always flow back to the source and mindset that has always set you apart.

1) The belief you are the best.
2) The confidence that you will overcome.
3) The strength to believe in your skills.
4) The heart that will never give in or say I cannot, because you know you can.

Your source will always win out! Stay connected to your source!"

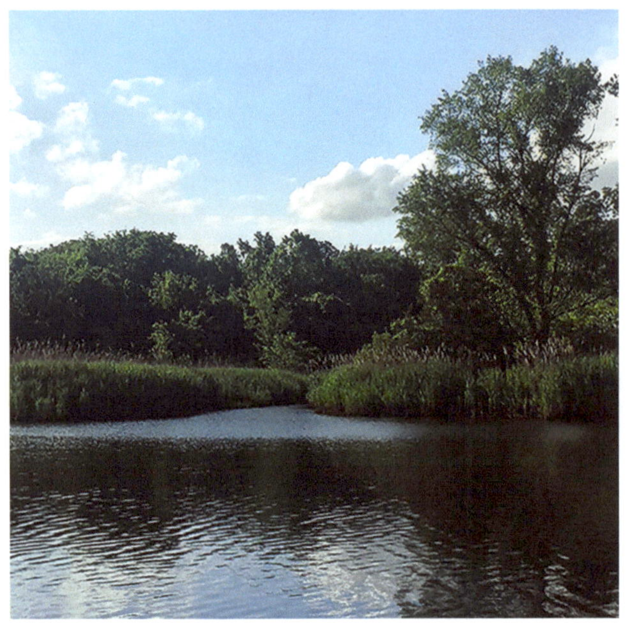

"Sometimes in life, you have to get out of the main stream and find your quiet stream."

"God knew your story the moment He created you. Therefore, He has already given you what you need today and tomorrow—your supply tank is full. Keep the pedal on the gas to arrive and thrive at the destination called hope, love and joy. Do not worry or be anxious for the life to come. He has prepared great things for your life ahead. May your heart jump with joy and the confidence within you shine brightly on your smiling face. He created you for this time. He has written your story and it is being revealed day by day. Stay strong and be patient. Stand in awe of His personal goodness. Know that what is to come will confirm His for you. Embrace each moment—seize and claim the daily blessings. Never allow self-doubt to float within your heart. Let Him work and stay confident, for He is doing something personally for you. Stay ready to receive what is to come."

"What anchors you? Find your anchor and strap it to your life. It will bring joy, strength, and contentment."

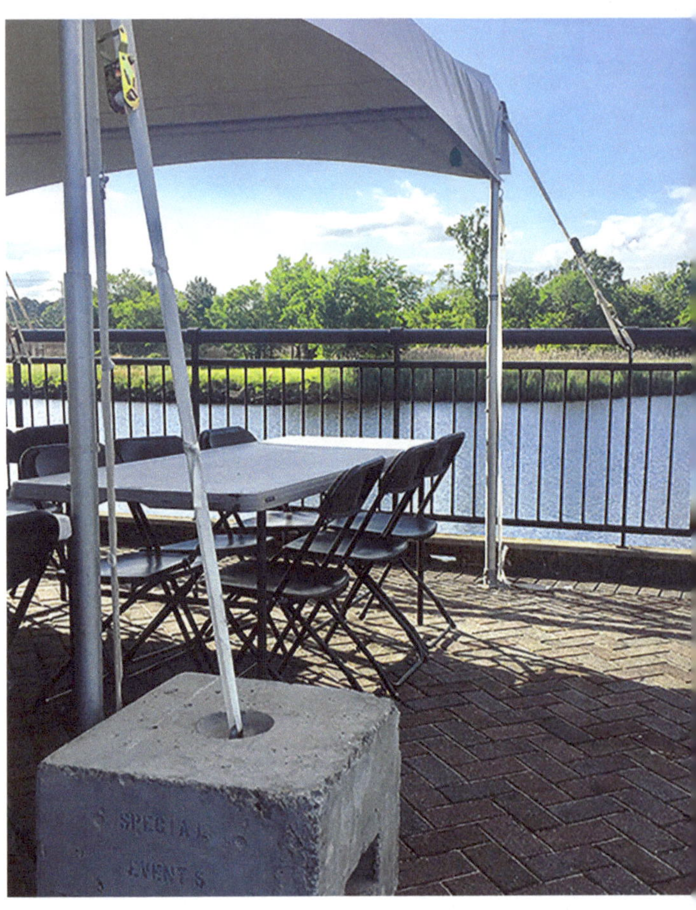

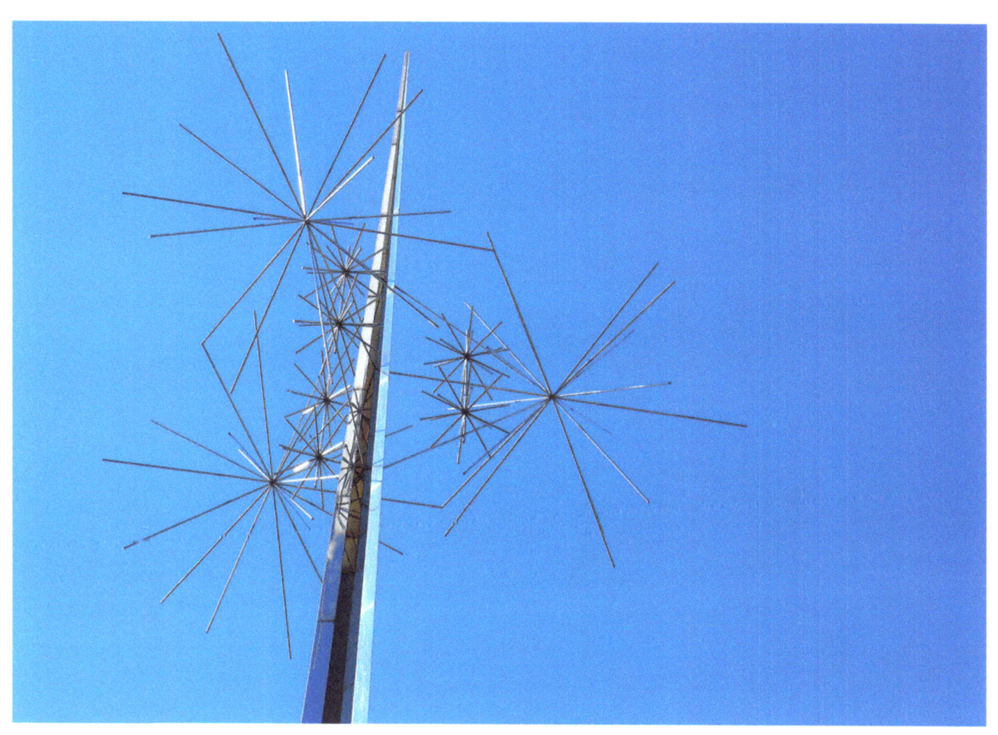

"Forgetting your past can release your new life and the future God has for you. Take steps to... Believe it! Embrace it! Emphasize it! Encourage it! Empower it! Energize it!"

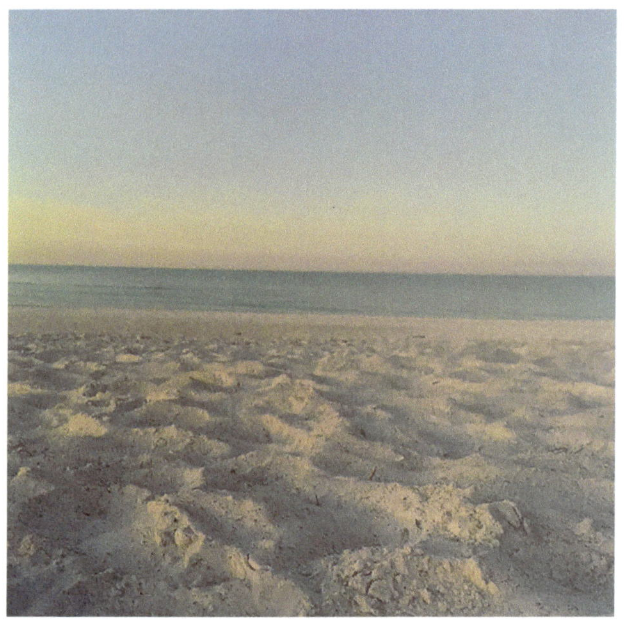

"Walk towards the source that will sustain
you! God is waiting!"

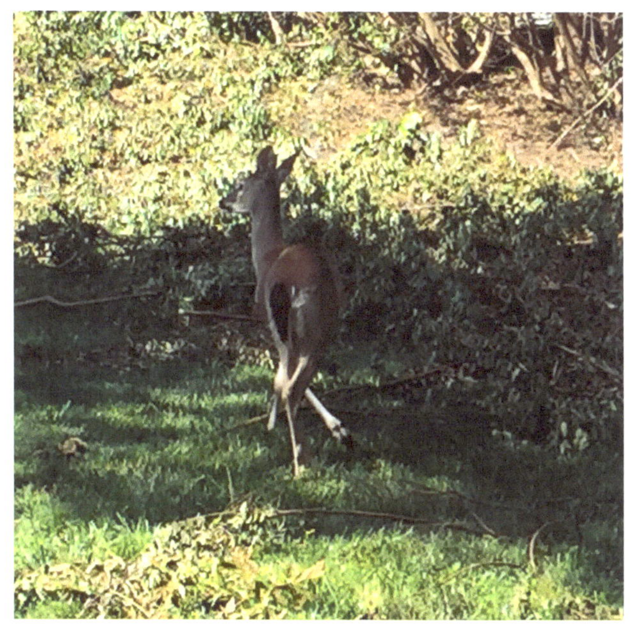

"Sometimes we can get confused on which way to turn. Remember to keep looking forward and you will soon see the goodness ahead."

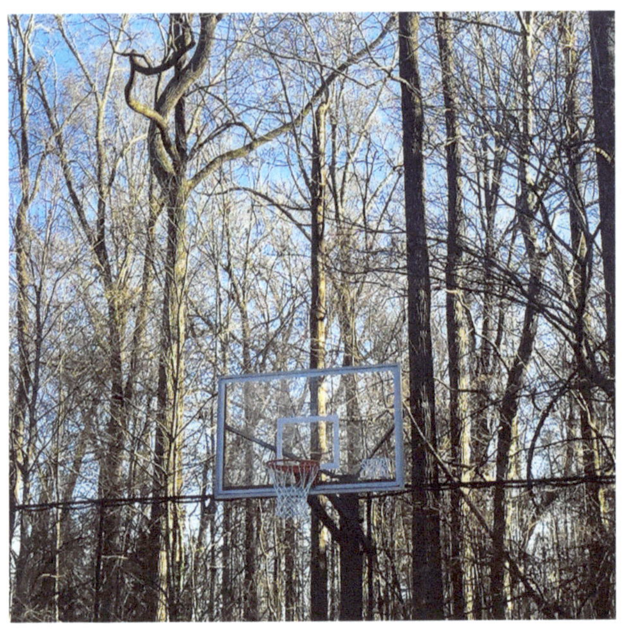

"This photo may appear lifeless. But if you add two things, a person and a ball, this picture will come alive. What two things can we add to our life?"

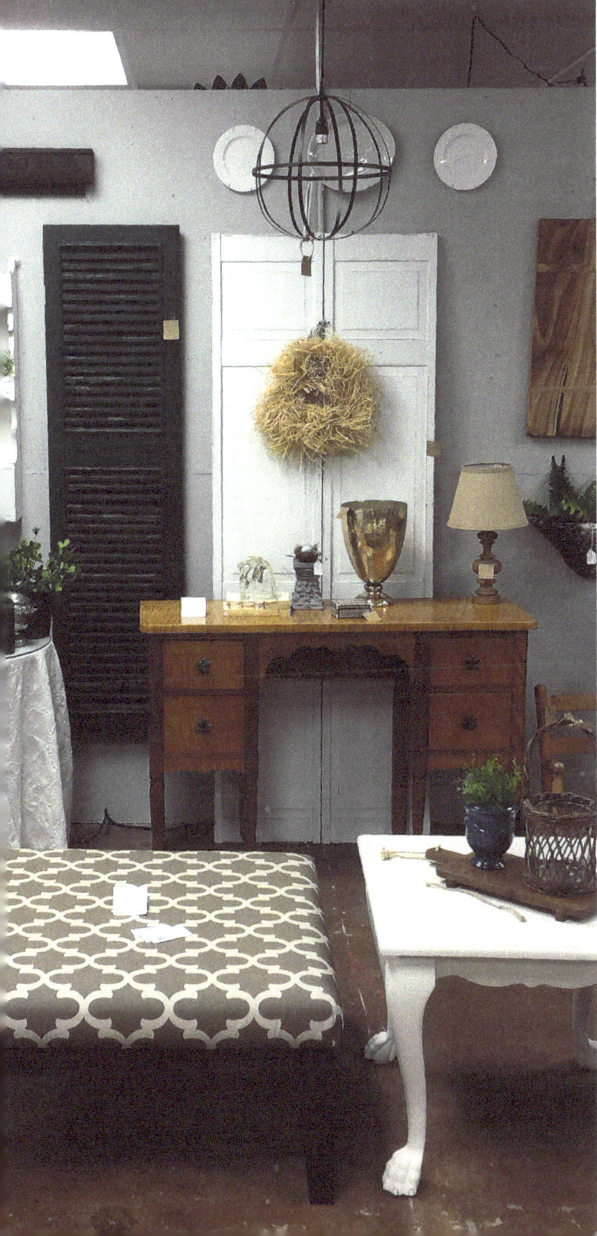

"It may appear old and out of place. When you splash some paint and clean up, you have something special. May this remind us that attention in the right areas of our life bring great rewards."

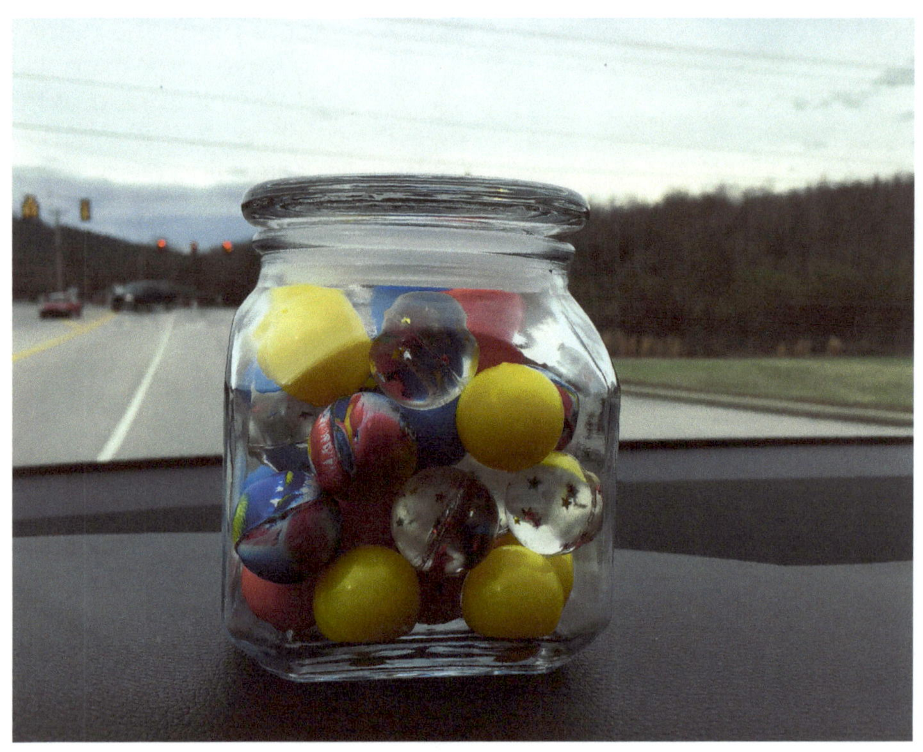

"Life can be a struggle and we wonder if we will bounce back and reach our pinnacle of success. Purchase some small bouncy balls and put them in a jar. This will help your remember that you will always bounce back."

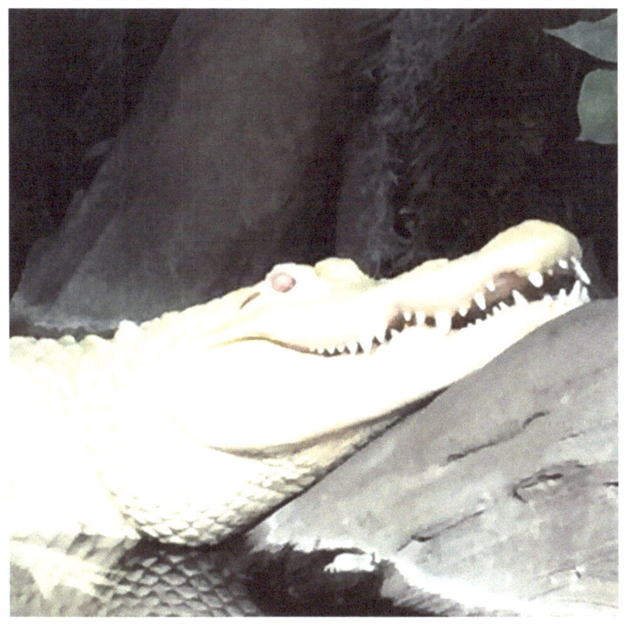

"God created us all differently but we all have purpose and meaning in this world. Never doubt your journey to find your purpose."

"Grab your phone and call the person that has been on your mind. Stop making excuses for not exercising your intuition. Never let it be said, 'I wish I would've called.' So, do it today."

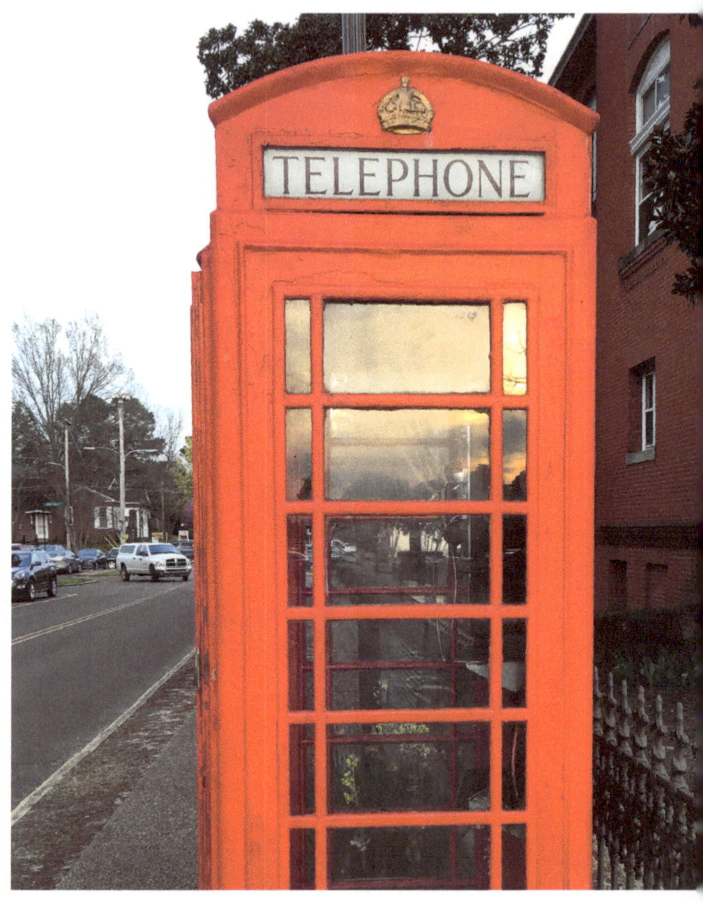

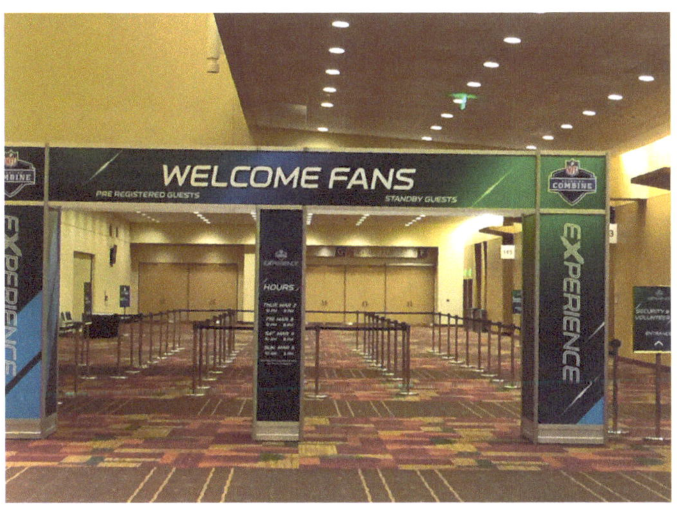

"Life is meant to be played out together. Find new fans and friends, join up and experience life serving each other and other people as well. The journey is more complete when you do it 1+1=2 versus 1+0=1."

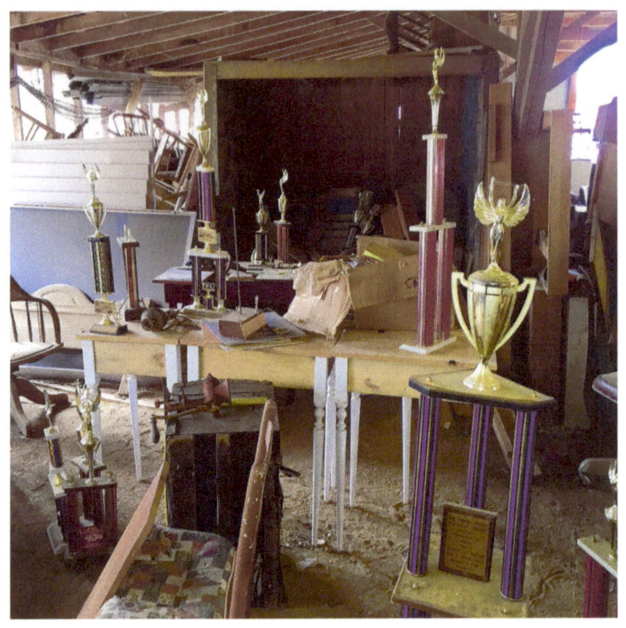

"I went to an old farm where all kinds of items were being sold. As I walked around, I came upon this shed that was not totally enclosed. Many trophies and awards were in the shed, constantly being exposed to the elements. I thought to myself, the treasure and awards on earth eventually rust and become junk. They have no purpose. Investing in others through time and commitment to serve, builds your legacy for generations. This legacy cannot be sold or purchased. It will never rust or be found years later in some old shed."

"Yes the road can be lonely and you may find yourself looking for encouragement. Keep going and follow the light on the path. You will arrive to your destination of peace."

"Going fast in life does not mean
you will be arriving fast."

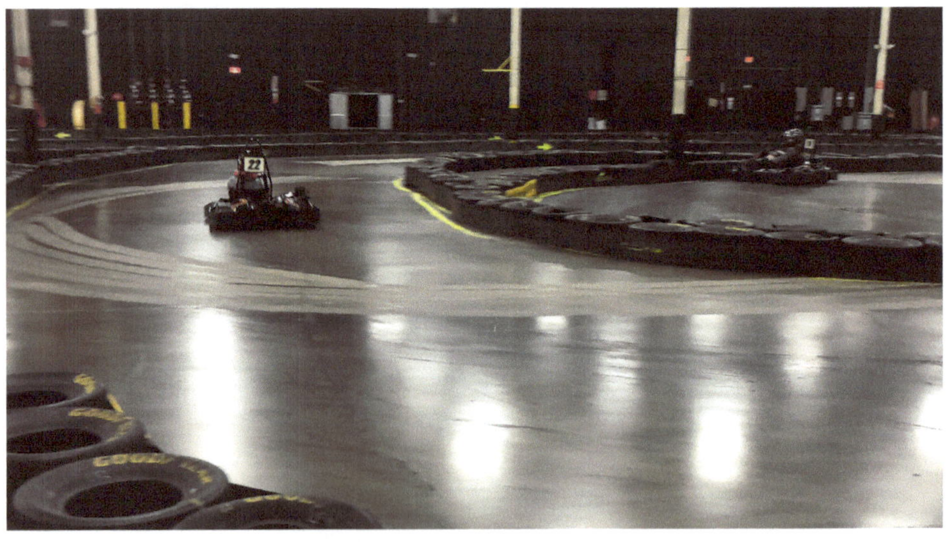

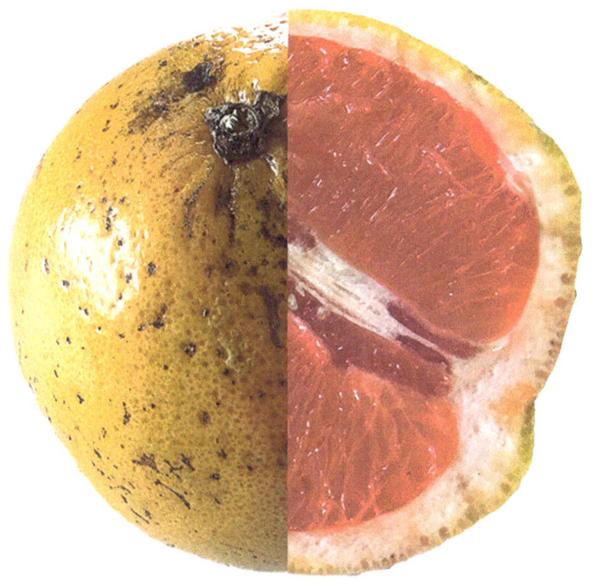

"Things may appear bad on the outside and many times we judge things strictly on appearance. This grapefruit tasted amazing, and I almost threw it away. But something said, 'Look inside'. I'm glad I did! May this remind us to look beyond the outward and focus inward."

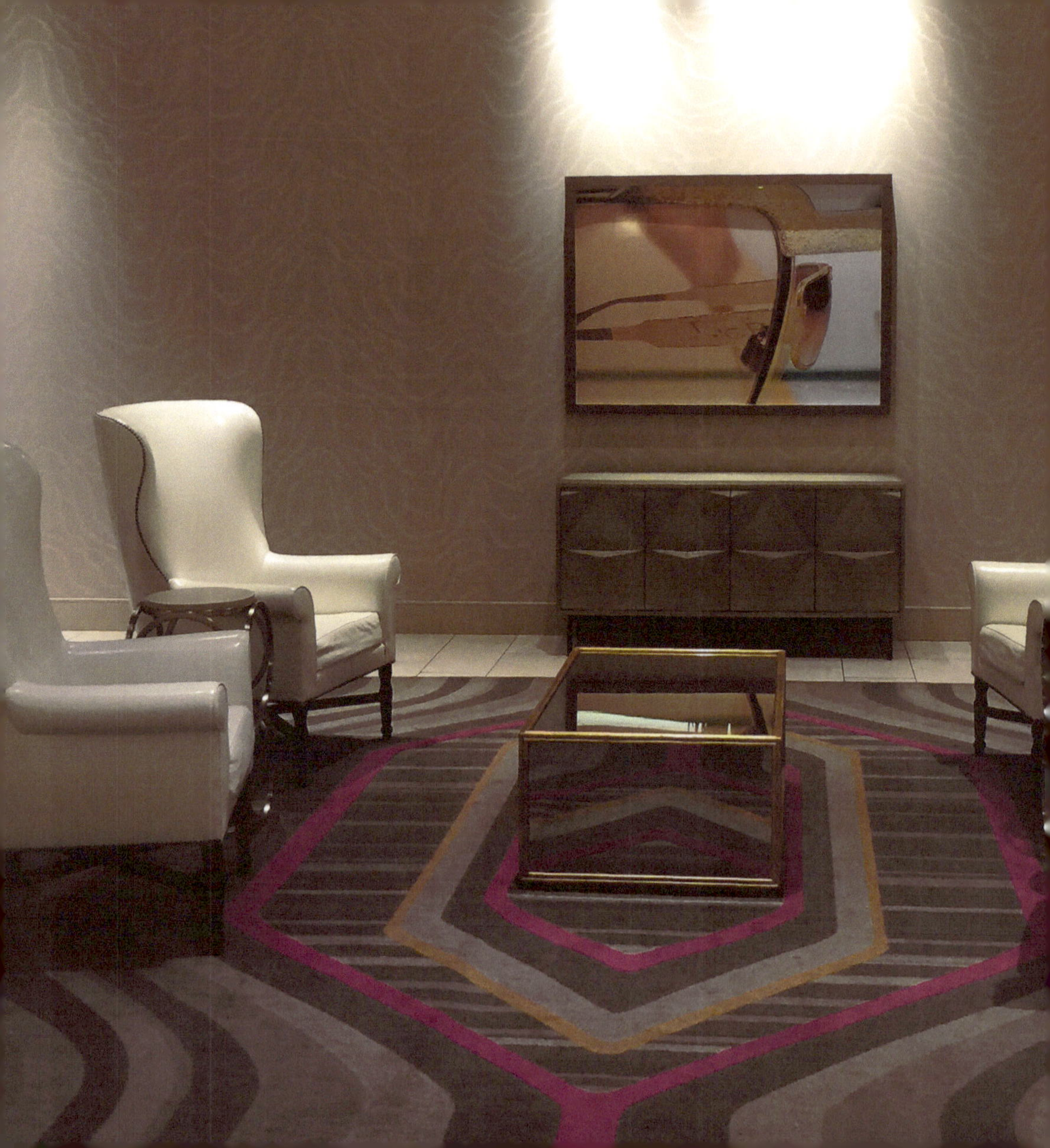

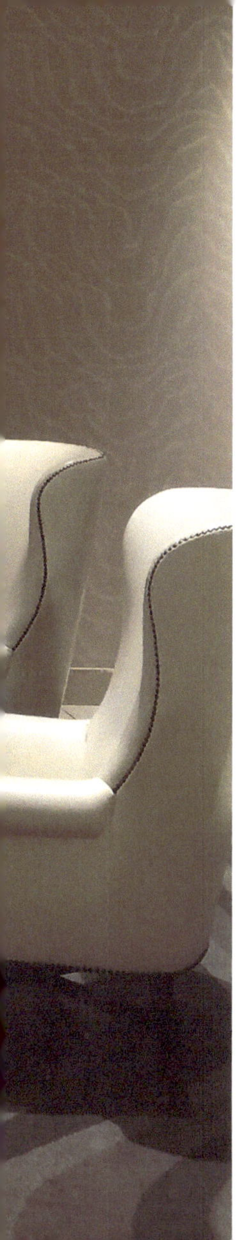

"Find a friend. Go sit and have a chat. Make the call and engage the conversation and time. Otherwise, the chairs and space have no benefit. We make it come alive."

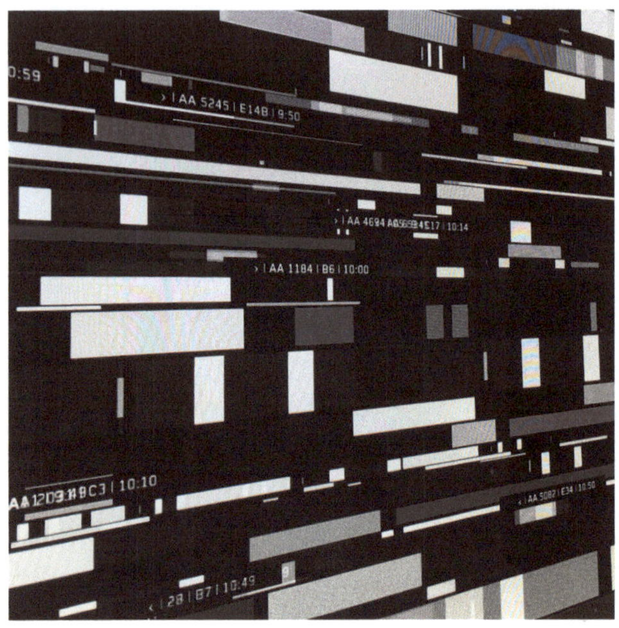

"The screen of life can go blank and we can lose our way. Know that it will come back on and the clarity you need will soon arrive."

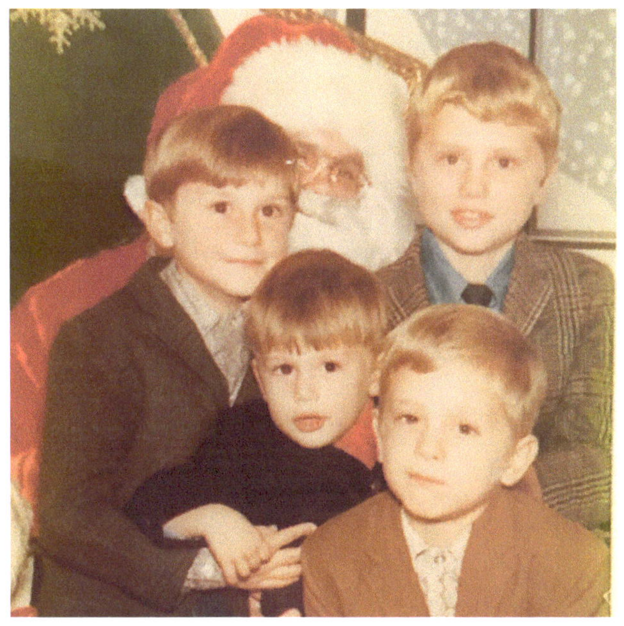

"Love everyday. You never know when you may lose someone close to you. Say, 'I love you' more than 'Goodbye' or 'Hello'."

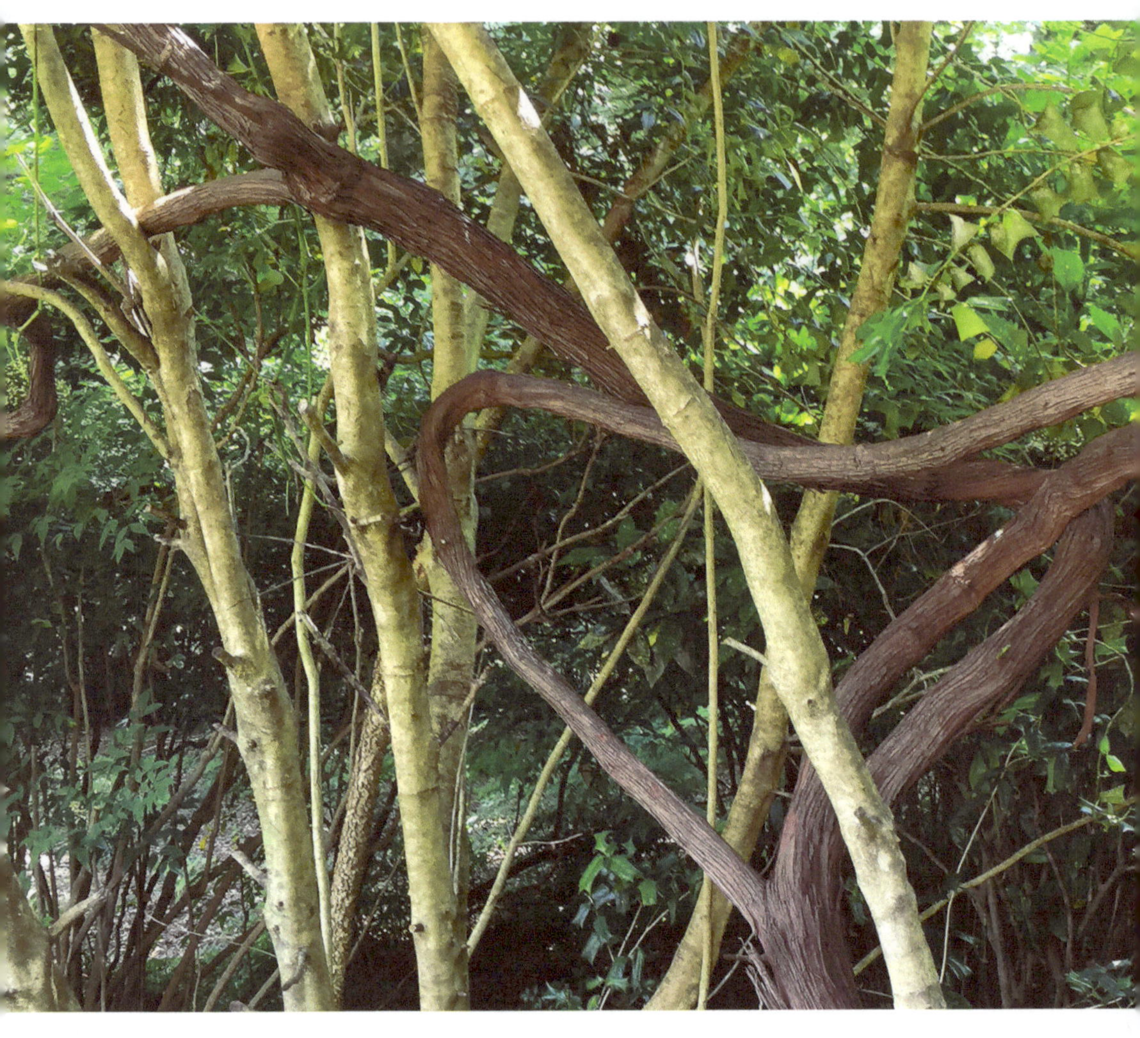

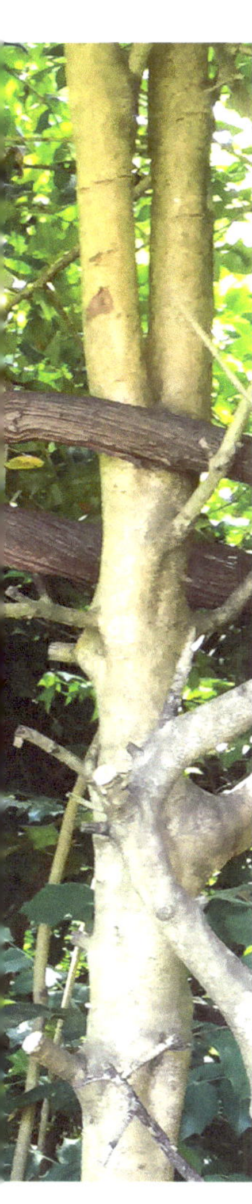

"If you clean out the clutter and trim a few things back, you may find the beauty within yourself."

"How do you get ahead? This seems to be the question of today. It's simple. Get started while others are sleeping. Rise 90 minutes early and see your success increase. I promise!"

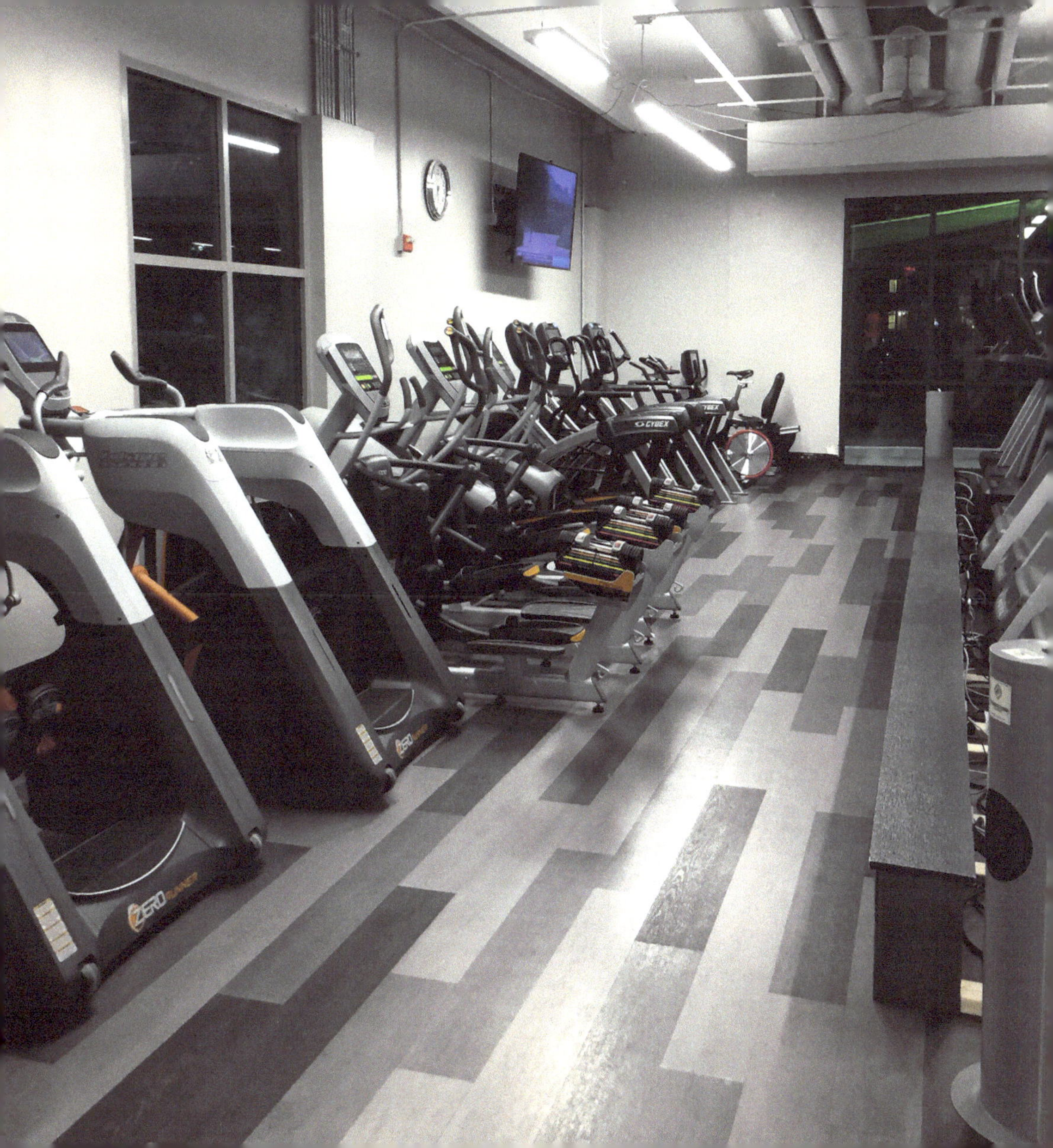
CYBEX

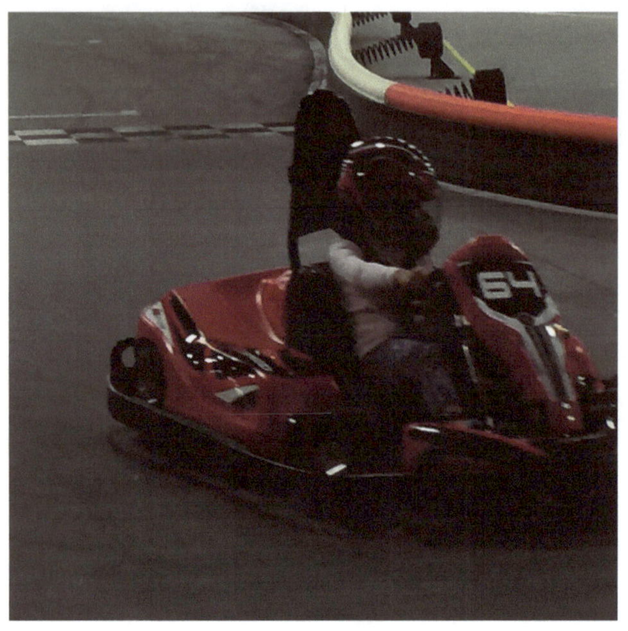

"Talent is intended to be developed. If you never step outside your comfort zone, you may find it challenging to discover your hidden talent, no matter your age."

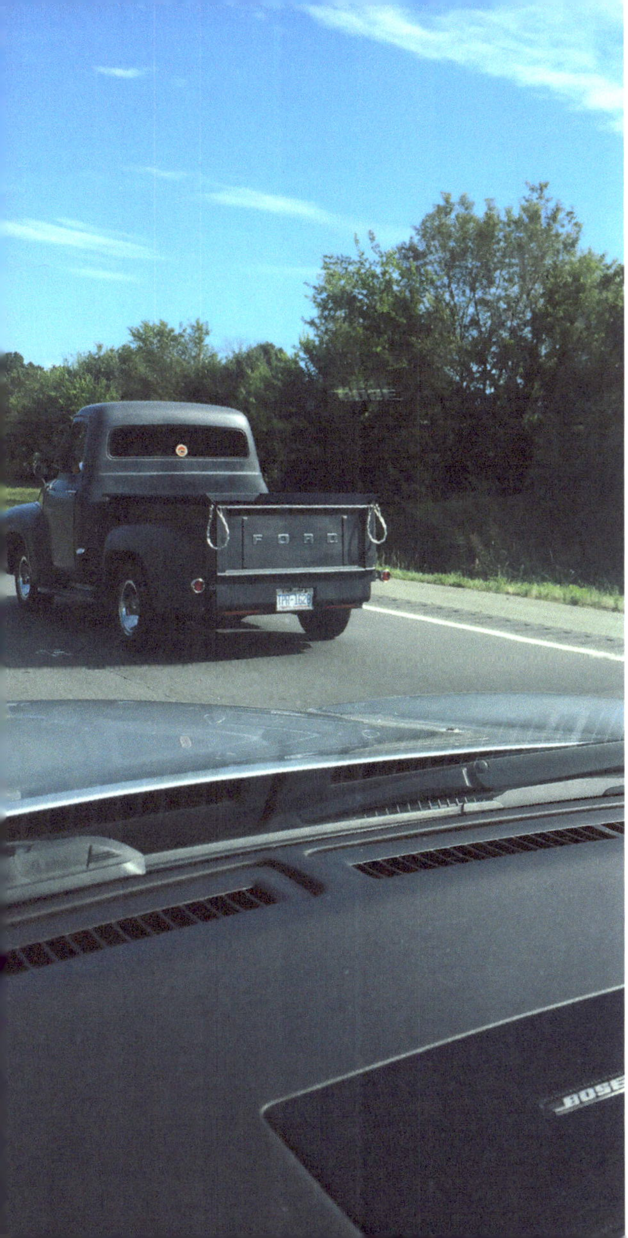

"Yesterday may have
contained great memories.
But, we have to let go and
build future memories."

"When God opens a door, move quickly. Just go! Yes, it takes courage and boldness to step forward, but know that you are never alone. He opened the door! He is waiting! Ready! Set! Go!"

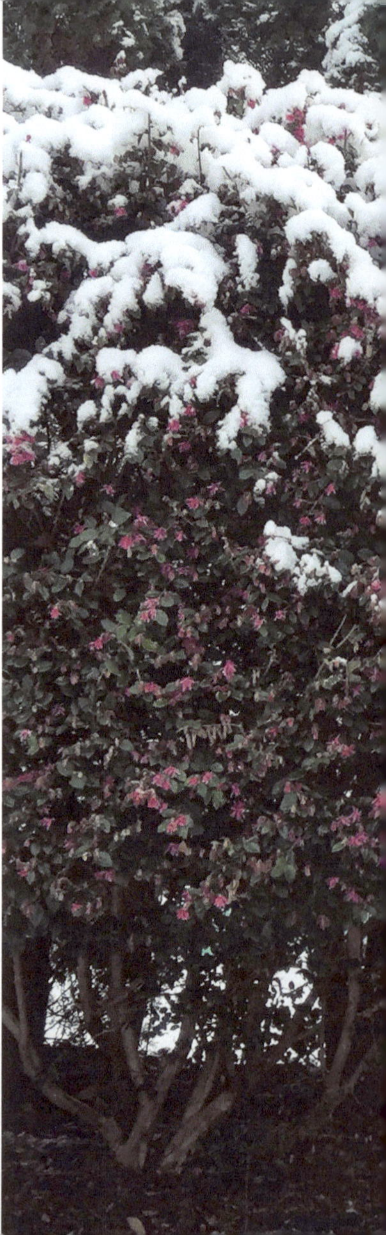

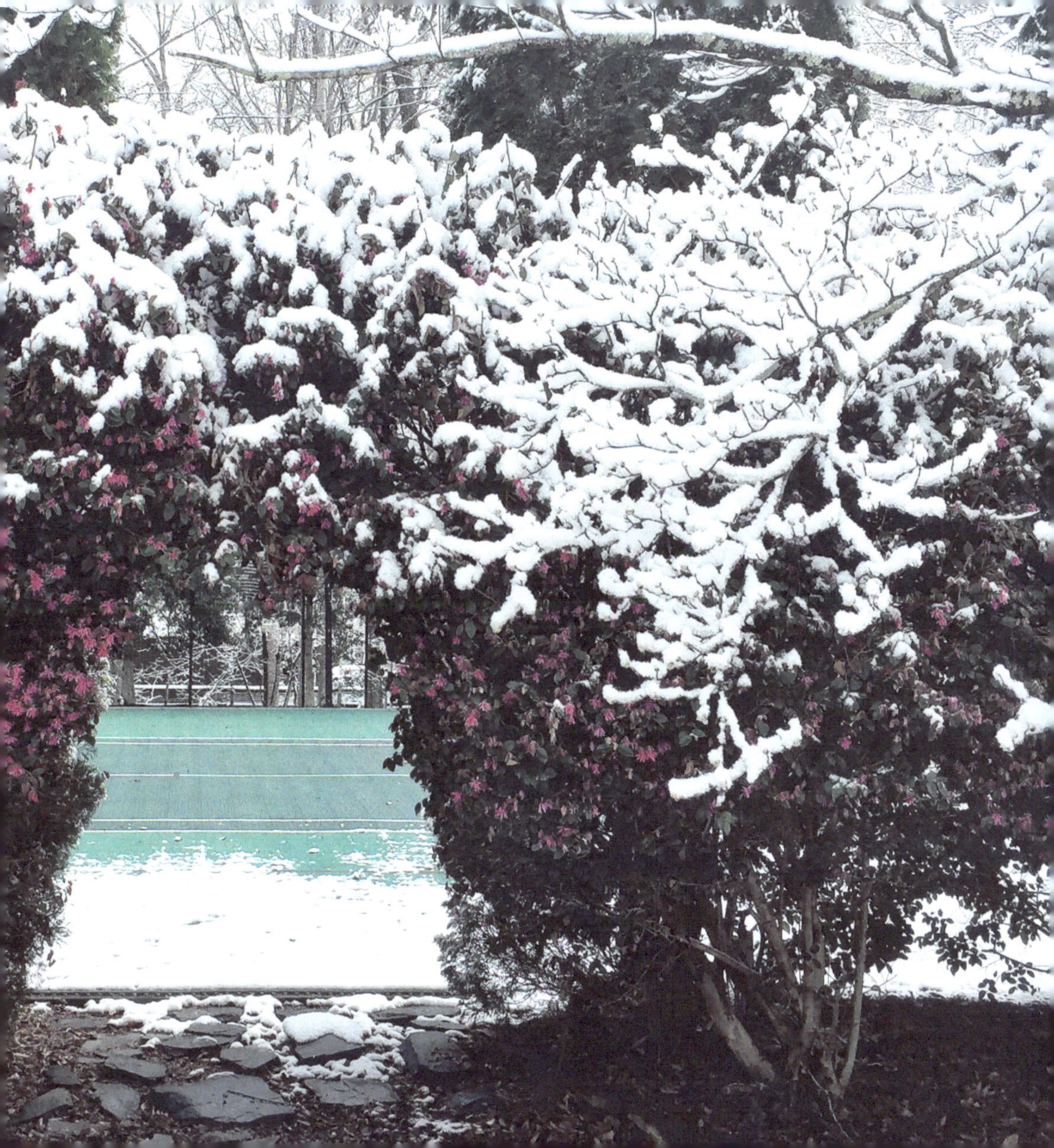

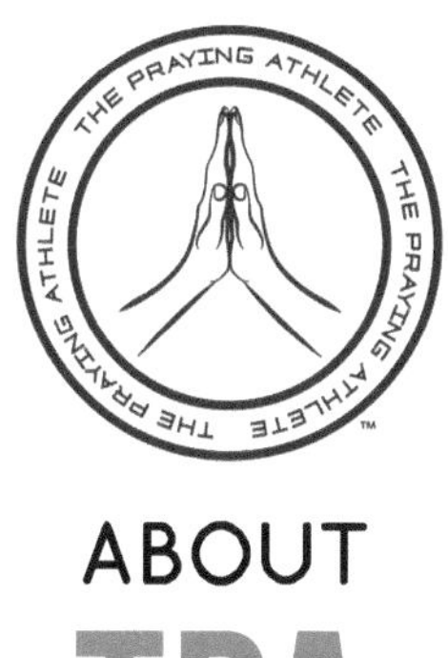

ABOUT TPA

The Praying Athlete is a movement that creates an organic culture of prayer through an uplifting community and authentic conversation.

For more information, visit our website **www.theprayingathlete.com**.

Follow us on social media.

 **@ThePrayingAthlete**

 **@Praying_Athlete**

 **@ThePrayingAthlete**

CHECK OUT OUR
THE PRAYING ATHLETE™
QUOTE BOOK SERIES

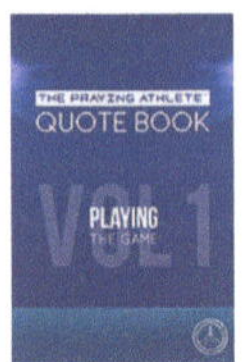

Our first volume of *The Praying Athlete Quote Book* addresses the topic of playing the game. Quotes and thoughts from Robert B. Walker, paired with Scripture from God's Word, allow readers to get a good idea about what playing a good game looks like.

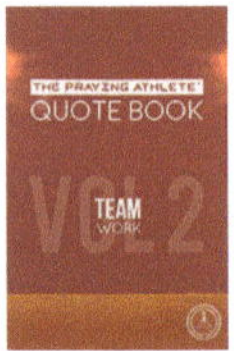

Our second volume of *The Praying Athlete Quote Book* addresses the topic of teamwork. Quotes and thoughts from Robert B. Walker, paired with Scripture from God's Word, allow readers to understand what it means to be a good teammate and surround yourself with people who lift you up.

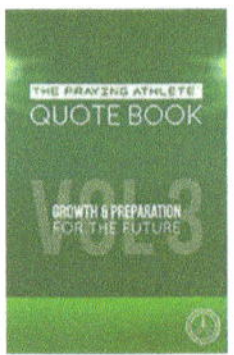

Our third volume of *The Praying Athlete Quote Book* addresses the topic of growth & preparation for the future. Quotes and thoughts from Robert B. Walker, paired with Scripture from God's Word, allow readers to know that even though the future is uncertain, there is a plan and purpose for everyone.

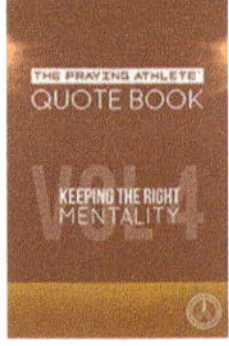

Our fourth volume of *The Praying Athlete Quote Book* addresses the topic of keeping the right mentality. Quotes and thoughts from Robert B. Walker allow readers to understand how staying in the right mindset can improve overall performance.

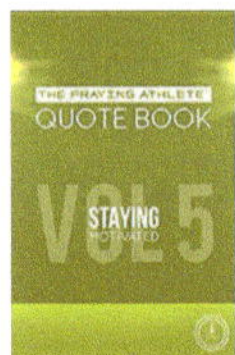

Our fifth volume of *The Praying Athlete Quote Book* addresses the topic of staying motivated. Quotes and thoughts from Robert B. Walker allow readers to become motivated to accomplish their goals, even when they feel they are not up to the task.

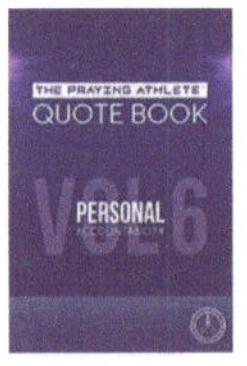

Our sixth volume of *The Praying Athlete Quote Book* addresses the topic of personal accountability. Quotes and thoughts from Robert B. Walker allow readers to think about how they can better themselves. Whether its ending a bad habit or saying no to anything that may hurt themselves or others, staying accountable will benefit one's character and performance.

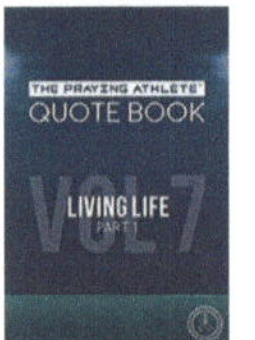

Our seventh volume of *The Praying Athlete Quote Book* addresses the topic of living life. This volume is the first part in a two part living life series. Quotes and thoughts from Robert B. Walker give readers a better understanding of how to live life to the fullest.

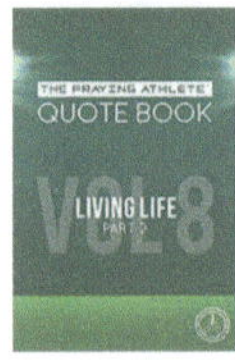

Our eighth volume of *The Praying Athlete Quote Book* addresses the topic of living life. This volume is the second part in a two part living life series. Quotes and thoughts from Robert B. Walker give readers a better understanding of how to live life to the fullest.

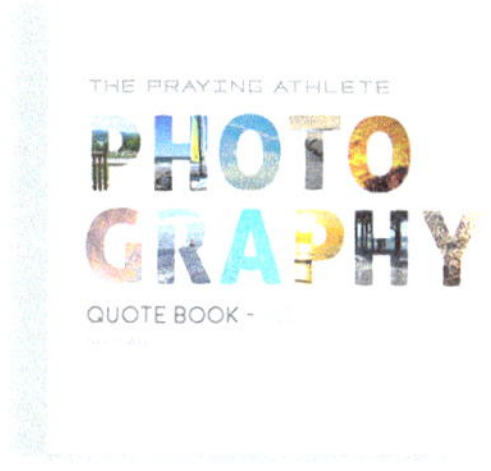

VOL. 1

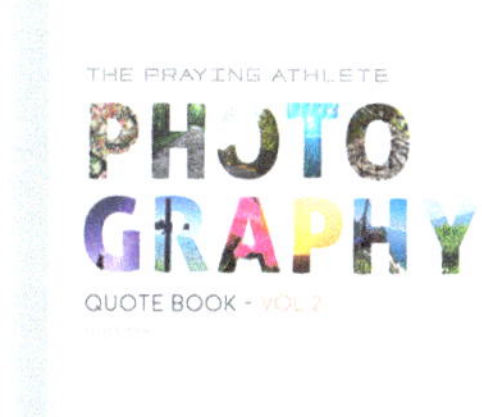

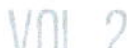

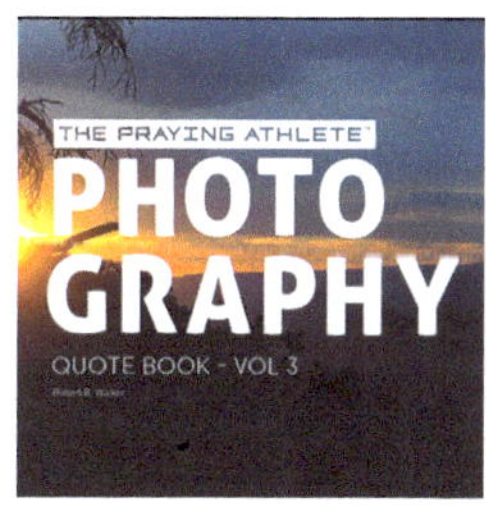

VOL. 3

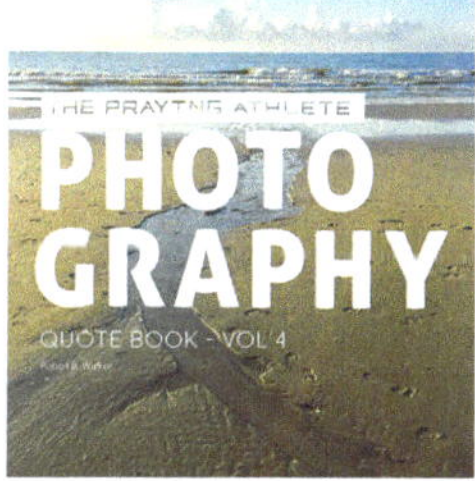

VOL. 4

*The Praying Athlete Photography Quote Book*s celebrate God's glory and magnificence through His creation. They contain photos taken by Robert B. Walker, paired with his words of wisdom, motivation, and inspiration.

www.ingramcontent.com/pod-product-compliance
Lightning Source LLC
LaVergne TN
LVHW070156110826
845147LV00002B/413

* 9 7 8 1 9 5 0 4 6 5 1 6 3 *